978-0-9894106-4-9

The Ink & Blood Dueling Society Doesn't Exist

Doesn't Exist

A Do-It-Yourself Guide to Hosting Writing Duel Events

By Capt. Jim "Blood" Markus

Illustrations By Charles Huth

THE INK & BLOOD DUELING SOCIETY

The ink & blood dueling society doesn't exist

There's no such thing as The Ink & Blood Dueling Society. It wasn't created in Chicago and, had it existed, I would have had nothing to do with it. A book about the inception of this particular secret society would provide such little value one might consider purchasing several dozen copies to use as kindling during the long, cold months of winter.

This book doesn't contain any information about The Ink & Blood Dueling Society. It doesn't contain any information about organizing, advertising, or producing theatrical writing shows. It contains zero secrets and it certainly doesn't suggest you create your own secret society. Such an attempt would be imprudent, impolite, and, frankly, impossible.

When I compiled these pages, my goal was to clear up any remaining rumors about these villainous literary events. There's no way to tell where they started, but it's not too late to put them to rest. If you demand to know more, know that this book has not been approved by The Ink & Blood Dueling Society. It couldn't have been, because that organization doesn't exist.

What is a writing duel?

While there's no such thing as The Ink & Blood Dueling Society, it would be ludicrous to suggest that there's no such thing as a writing duel. Of course there's no clandestine cadre of linguistic duelists. That doesn't mean nobody ever gets together to compete in literary combat. Let's start with that. What is a writing duel?

Picture two writers, Irene and Jebediah. Irene walks into your local cafe with her eyes half closed and smiles when she smells freshly-brewed coffee. Jebediah sits alone at a table in the corner. His fingers shake as he drinks from his impressively small glass, and his eyes dart from his computer to the barista to the door. "Four cortados in an hour," he explains.

"Duel?" Irene asks.

Jebediah opens his laptop, puts his fingers over the keys, and waits. "What's the prompt?"

"Secrets," Irene responds as she opens her own laptop and sits down. She's at Jebediah's table, facing him.

"Time?"

"Ten minutes."

The two writers immediately go silent. Their eyes focus on their computer screens, and they type without pause.

If you've been using your imagination during this fictional exchange, you just witnessed the simplest form of writing duel. In short, writing duels are shared writing prompts with time limits.

The duelists are writers, the weapons are computers, and the dueling fields are screens. In most cases after the duels, the writers share their works aloud and agree on which piece turned out better. In the following chapters, we'll cover the rituals and tactics that arose from this general concept.

There are three types of duels: Personal Duels, Dueling Events, and Large Shows. Each of these serves a different audience, and each has a slightly different format. Personal duels are performed only for the writers involved. Dueling events are performed for small audiences, and large events are performed for enormous crowds of people.

Personal duels

You've already imagined a personal duel. These types of events can happen all the time. Imagine you're relaxing with a lifelong friend. This is one of those long-time hangouts, where neither of you made any specific plans other than to be doing the same thing at the same time in the same place, wherever that might be.

Are you picturing this? Your friend insists that you should do something, anything. You're both writers, after all. Isn't there something you could both do at the same time, in the same place? Yes. Of course there is. You both have laptops, and you enjoy putting words in various orders. Your friend pulls out her smartphone and sets a timer for ten minutes. You spot a potted cactus in the corner of the room and, thinking it looks out of place next to an aquarium of fish, you decide on your prompt. "Cactus," you say. Your friend starts the timer, and you both start writing. Once the timer beeps, you both stop. That's a writing duel. Neat.

Is there more to it? That depends on who you ask. Some people think complexity improves the experience like sriracha sauce improves every dish to which it's added. These people usually think rituals and masks offer excitement to the competition. Other people think eggs are just fine without sriracha, Sarah. Why does everything need to involves rituals and masks with you? It's just fine for eggs to taste like eggs. Geeze.

Dueling events

For Irene and Jebediah, who began their imaginary writing duel earlier, writing duels required none of the pomp of a secret society. They met at a coffee shop and began writing almost immediately. Members of The Ink & Blood Dueling Society, if that organization existed, would almost certainly take it a few steps further. Their events are dueling events. They involve more than just two writers.

The Ink & Blood Dueling Society's writing duel events would take place in front of live audiences. They would include masks and chanting, cloaks and quills. Dueling events entertain more than the two competing writers. They were designed to appeal to a niche audience of literature lovers.

If that sounds like your kind of thing, you're going to love this next part. In fact, I'll tease you with an answer before you even hear the question.

You.

The answer is you.

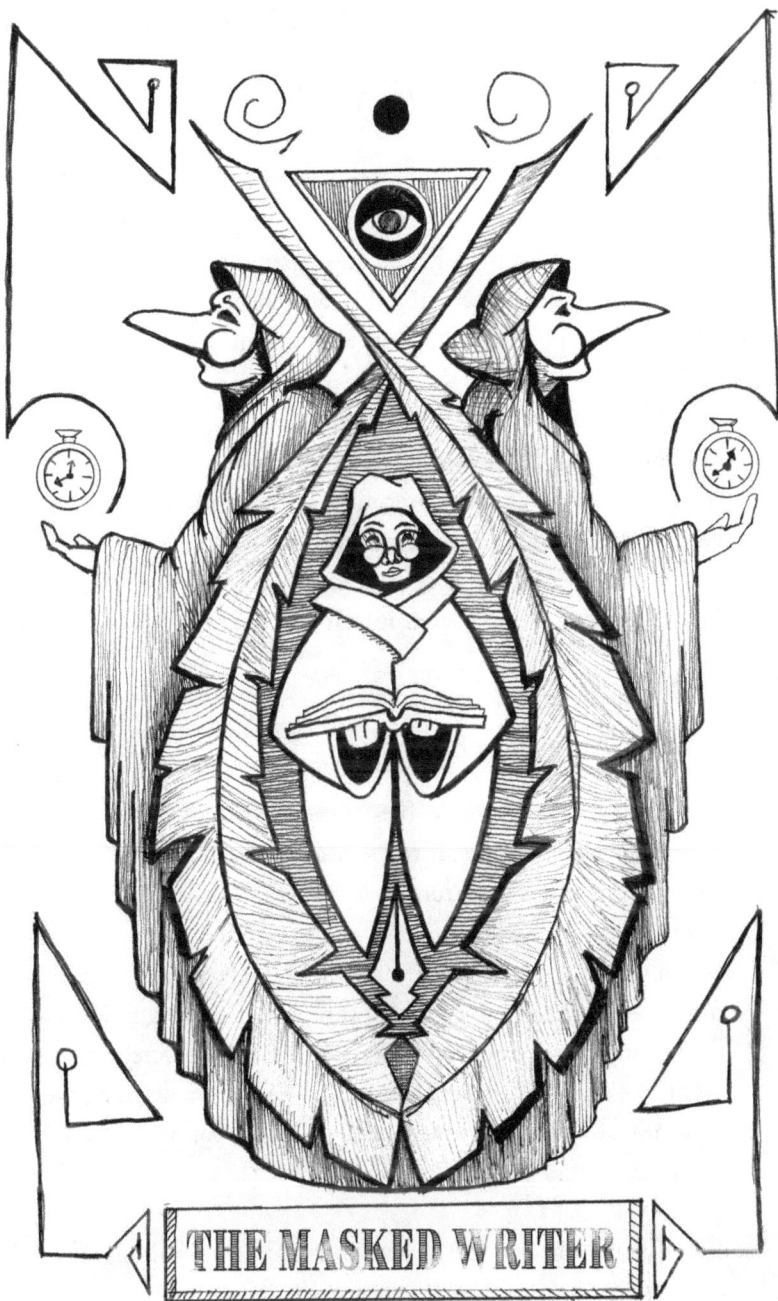
THE MASKED WRITER

Who participates in a writing duel?

It's tempting to say writing duelists come in all shapes and sizes, but that's not exactly true. Traditionally, writing duelists have always been at least vaguely human shaped. They're almost always tall enough to jump over a thimble, and they're almost never too large to fit inside a medium-sized auditorium.

You don't need an invitation to attend a writing duel. If you're the kind of person who doesn't do anything without an invitation, then you must have a very peaceful social life. You also must get very cold during the winter, waiting for someone to open the door for you to go inside your house. You don't need an invitation because this is your invitation. You can do this right now.

Where to find writers

Where do you find writers? They're everywhere. We're everywhere. Chances are, if you're reading this book, you're a writer. Congratulations. You're everywhere. Woah.

When we first started organizing writing duels, we had some trouble finding enough people to compete. The thing is, it's not the writing that scares people away. At our totally secret writing event, the scary part is the crowd. Your work is on display as you type. You see, we weren't just organizing duels for ourselves. We organized them for public consumption.

When there's an audience to read and react to your thoughts, everything changes. That's especially true when they're encouraged to shout at you while you work. Dozens of people watch you introduce your character and create a fulfilling plot arc in ten minutes.

Some people won't like what you write. People might make corny jokes about your ideas or worse, your mistakes. There's also a guy in the second row who loudly calls out every typo, and he's a more helpful audience member than the one who keeps asking you to introduce a velociraptor into your space western.

That's what you're up against when you invite writers to participate in a live writing duel. We are observant creatures, writers. And we recognize potential moments of embarrassment right away. The writers who don't recognize these potential challenges either haven't been warned or lack the mental limitations of mere mortals.

If you don't already have a few friends in your local writing community, start there. You want to participate in a writing duel? Start with people who write all the time. You might find them in the same coffee shop where we already agreed you're reading this book.

Want to draw an interesting group? Place an ad in your local paper that reads something like this:

Writers needed: Local secret society seeks talented, tenacious writers for literary battles among community of vicious, more talented rivals. Masks welcomed but rarely required.

It'll be more secretive if you don't mention where to send inquiries, but you'll have more responses if you end your advertisement with a P.O. box or something.

Here's the thing, it's much easier to find writers when you gather a small crowd at your event. Literary events tend to attract people who want to participate in literary events. Get a small corral of writers for your first few shows and mine your audience for more talent.

The best participants

Once you have a live writing event, there's no shortage of potential participants. Some people will come to your event only because they want to write. There's nothing wrong with that, especially if they're talented writers, but the best participants are always fans of the show.

There's another benefit to pulling talent from your audience. Not only are they less likely to be distracted or dismayed by the noise, they're also smarter and more physically attractive. They smell like chocolate chip oatmeal cookies, and they taste like hot cocoa.

Whether you import your writers from three towns away or elevate them from your own group of fans, it's important to vet talent before you put it on the big screen. The best duelists can make you laugh as they create compelling content. They can also usually tell full stories quickly. Said another way, strong duelists know how to get laughs without sacrificing plot.

Where to look for the best writing duelists:

Find writers who want to write. If you can't find professionals or talented amateurs, look for anyone who tells stories for a living. Those might be the people who go to live storytelling events, especially those who work without notes. You can also approach people who work in comedy.

If you find a professional writer, they should already know how to tell a story. If you find a professional writer who also works in comedy, they should have all the skills they need to win every writing duel ever. If you are a professional writer who works in comedy, get my contact information and send offers for staff writing gigs.

Writing duels as comedic entertainment

Writing duel events are a form of theater, but don't let the word Theater scare you away. Magicians, mimes, and improv students are also kinda sorta members of the theater community.

Improvisers and writing duelists share many traits. Both perform in front of audiences without defined plans. They may approach their shows with general forms and ideas, but the best performers find their work in the moment. They feed off their environments, crowd reactions, and unexpected prompts.

Literate improvisers are natural writing duelists. These performers already have experience standing in front of a crowd. They already have experience playing with each other and playing with their audiences. All of this experience serves their abilities as writing duelists. I'm not sure I can say the same about writing duelists. The best writing duelists may be playful enough to win a crowd, but they may not have the confidence that comes with time spent on stage. Our writers stay hidden, so they don't need to be extroverts to participate.

Writing duels as "legitimate theater"

Some people take everything seriously. They strain to find the underlying meaning behind the media they consume, delighting in patterns and jumping at opportunities to quickly make connections. These are the kind of people who, while trying to write a book about writing duels, order a made-from-scratch chicken pot pie and pause to deliberate over a bite. They don't deliberate over every bite, but this latest one had a few small chicken bones in it. The type of people who take everything seriously might ponder the meaning of such a bone before they returned to their work. Chicken bones, one might argue, show that the pie was made from scratch. Chicken bones, consequently, are what it's all about.

There's nothing wrong with being serious about your work just like there's nothing wrong with being serious about pot pie. Just don't suck all the joy out of it while you study the details.

Enjoy your pie. Enjoy your writing duels. If you can appreciate both, it doesn't matter if you're an especially serious person or an especially silly one.

Why do writers duel?

Asking why writers duel is like asking why a Captain must go down with her ship. It's like asking why doves crack under light interrogation or why the sun disappears so quickly when winter shows up. That is to say, it's a fine question and you shouldn't be forced to accept "just because" as an answer.

Different writers duel for different reasons. Some use it as a motivation technique. When we held our first practice duels in a coffee shop in Chicago's Logan Square neighborhood, we all had our own projects. The goal of the duel was just to get writing. Our stories could have turned into short stories, or they could have been immediately forgotten. Whenever I felt inhibited, a feeling lesser captains sometimes call "writer's block," I'd challenge my friends to a writing duel.

The immediate time constraint gave me adequate reason to write. Seeing my companions write also spurred my competitive side. Often those writing duels turned onto short stories. I've revised, submitted, and published some without adding much to their length. I even got to read two duel-inspired stories on stage at a "we're known for long form" improv theater in Chicago.

That's a circuitous way of saying this: One reason people write is for motivation, but that's not the only reason. Some writers, many writers, enjoy competition. They want to sharpen their skills and defeat their opponents. They want the glory of an audience's appreciation.

Because we unmask only one winner at each of our events, only one writer earns a moment of fame in front of our audience. That's what inspires competitive duelists to compete again and again.

Why we never advertise who's writing

One of the fundamental reasons we use masks to hide the identities of our writers is protection. We ask people to compete in front of a live, aggressive audience for laughs. We don't want to embarrass anyone whose work suffered because of the environment. We don't advertise our writers because we want them to compete without concern over their personal brand. Some of our writers are published authors. Others produce events of their own.

Oscar Wilde said, "Man is least himself when he talks in his own person. Give him a mask, and he will tell you the truth." That's true with writing duels as well. We want to see the raw, unpolished talent of our writers. That's why we come to these shows. Give the writers anonymity, and they'll be comfortable enough to write sci-fi erotica. Isn't that what it's all about?

Anonymity comes with a few challenges as well. Some writers get stage fright, even if they're not going to be on stage. Sometimes they don't take their commitments seriously, either. There's no easy way to tell a writer that they've betrayed your trust, that they've let down an audience, and that they'll never be allowed to participate again. So, we basically never do. We tried to enforce no-show rules, but we really liked the people who wanted to write with us. That's why we ended up using some of the people who burned us once in the past.

That's not to say we're pushovers. Our writing duels are pretty much the greatest thing that happens in an independent bookstore after closing hours (before the ghosts start roaming around the paranormal section). We like what we do, and we want to work with people who value it too.

After we started our show, lots of people wanted to participate. We started to vet writers before allowing them to participate. I was especially surprised by how many people approached me, asking to write at one of our shows without ever having seen one of our shows. I'm getting sidetracked here. If you want to know more about who writes in our duels and how we choose them, check out the earlier "Who Participates in a Writing Duel" section of this book.

Who attends writing duels?

These events draw all sorts of fun people. People who like literary events usually like these types of things. People who are into modern art, especially performance art, if they existed, would like these shows. These are performative shows. They're comedic and theatrical and strange. Said another way, we made our show for pro-wrestling fans. Yes. That bears repeating.

More than anyone else, we made our show for pro-wrestling fans.

Our theater is built on lies.

That's only 80% false. When we created our secret society of writers, we did so with a concept we borrowed from pro wrestlers. When I say "borrowed," I mean we smashed pro wrestling in the head with a metal folding chair and tore it from their loosened grip. The concept we stole is called kayfabe, and it has been a vital part of our events from the very beginning.

If you don't know what kayfabe is, just think of pro wrestling shows. In those shows, wrestlers assume larger-than-life personalities and present pre-written storylines as if they were reality. The audience knows they're fake, but they play along. They cheer for it. They come back to follow along because they recognize the characters even though they know the characters aren't real people. That's kayfabe.

Our first hosts and producers all assumed fictionalized identities. We built fake characters, spent way too much time writing fake histories, and then presented them to a bewildered audience. It was fun for us, and it allowed us to develop more theatrical productions. I claimed to be captain of a pirate ship, and would you believe nobody ever once called me out on this little fib? Our triumvirate also included my rival, Lord C. Byron Taylor, and Dr. Lottie Jenkins, a professor who insisted she was the best inventor in the world (she just happened to make things explode).

Eventually we brought in actors and comedians to host. Those new additions to our show kept the kayfabe elements, and now our audience expects it. One host closes each of his events with a sort of ritualized prayer. It's half corny and half serious. It's also completely brilliant. He took one of our most celebrated concepts and used it to formalize an end to the show.

Our audience is funnier than you are.

Letting the audience in on the joke also acts as an invitation. We offer some tongue-in-cheek openings because it helps everyone loosen up. Sometimes we plant people in the crowd to start chants. It doesn't take long before these chants take on a life of their own. For example, our audience all shouts out the countdown as each round ends. When the writers have less than ten seconds left, everyone counts the numbers down aloud. We do this to put extra pressure on the writers and to remind the audience that something new is about to happen. The stories will be read aloud in a moment.

Other chants and tropes grew organically. Common themes form and audiences start to work together in their feedback. People shout to each other in the crowd, but they're always drawn back into the story. You'll learn to recognize the dynamics of crowd feedback when you host a few shows of your own. These depend on your audience, of course, but they also depend on the format of the show you create.

Some audiences have powerful voices, and often they're as witty as the writers. That makes sense, right? Many of them are writers themselves.

How do you win a writing duel?

There are different strategies for different types of duels. If you're competing in personal duels, you can't lose. There's nothing on the line with personal duels. You either write something, or you don't. If you write something, cheers. If you don't, what is your partner going to do? They might chide you for your inability to put words on paper, but they aren't going to quill you to death.

Writing duel events are different. There's a real risk of death at those things, or so I hear. You'll need to do your best at a show, so pay attention or the audience will throw unsharpened pencils at you.

Everything depends on your audience.

The audience is the heart of the event, and they pump energy through the show so everything can function. What does that mean to you? It means you shouldn't ask so many rhetorical questions, Sarah. Just write to please your audience. Here are a few strategies to consider when you sit behind the curtain for the first time. I've broken them down by different types of events. I've seen all of these in person, but it's by no means a complete list. Your audience might be totally different than any of these, and that's totally cool. Every crowd is different just like every event is different. Here are some of the types of crowds that showed up during the first two years of writing duels in Chicago.

The Fun Crowd

Every audience can be fun, but some crowds will enjoy themselves just by showing up. They aren't concerned with the quality of the writing, they don't mind if someone makes a mistake and, just as importantly, they're not loyal to any one writer.

There are a few quick ways to identify this crowd. First, they're loud. Of all the groups described here, this is the one with the most frequent shouts and the loudest laughs. Fun crowds just want to be entertained, and they make it easy. They laugh at each other's jokes. They make jokes about the other jokes they hear. There are so many jokes you'll need a broom to sweep away the shattered remains of your more fragile audience members.

If you hear someone in the crowd heckle another member of the crowd (and the rest of the audience laughs), that's a clue you found The Fun Crowd.

Benefits of the Fun Crowd: These events always go well. Fun crowds make it very easy to run a show because they entertain each other. They laugh and joke and vote with their friends. If your show runs late, or if you have performers who fall a few minutes behind, The Fun Crowd will talk and drink while they wait.

Challenges of the Fun Crowd: Don't expect the person who wrote the most eloquent story to win the event. The Fun Crowd doesn't want literature. In most cases, they want laughs. They're also tough to corral when it's time to vote. Have you ever tried to get a horde of pirates to board an enemy ship at the height of a battle? Some of your audience will rush toward the voting cup, while others continue to sling barbs toward their least favorite stories.

Hosts may not be able to easily calm the loudest audience members when it's time to read, and sometimes that's alright.

How writers respond to The Fun Crowd: These groups can also be polarizing for writers. Some writers, especially those who feel uncomfortable with aggressive shouting aimed at their precious work, clam up in front of The Fun Crowd. Other writers hear the sarcastic wit of the audience and use the charged atmosphere as an invitation to be goofy. If you want to practice for a Fun Crowd, tough luck. You can do all the coffee-shop duels you want. Nothing compares to the real thing in front of a live, loud audience.

Strategies for a Fun Crowd show: Unlike other audiences, the Fun Crowd doesn't demand high quality writing. They demand laughter. Keep this in mind when you book your event. The Fun Crowd appreciates a confident, funny host. They prefer writers who interact with the audience in their stories. Book a comedian to host. Book comedy writers to write. Then, expect a relaxed atmosphere.

Fun Crowds tend to enjoy loose-format shows. We're starting fifteen minutes late? No problem. The show begins with a funny intro without much explanation? No problem. The winning writer broke format and wrote a poem that made the crowd laugh? No worries at all. Keep this one loose and fun.

The Scholarly Crowd

Every audience can be scholarly, but there's a certain type of audience that comes to our events that just wants to read strong literature. The Scholarly Crowd doesn't often make as much noise as other crowds, but they're not completely silent either. Expect to hear well-timed wit during these writing duel events, but don't expect the same kind of banter or silliness you might get with other groups.

If you hear someone make a genuine request for a well-structured plot, that's a clue The Scholarly Crowd showed up at your event.

Benefits of the Scholarly Audience: Smart, quiet audiences may not laugh as loudly or as often as other crowds, but they usually get better-quality stories. Our hidden writers almost always want to please the crowd, and loud audiences often cause writers to go for quick laughs. Quieter crowds judge duels by the full readings, and they'll usually vote for a well-written piece over something that caused a couple laughs. As an added bonus, the pieces written during these events can often be used afterward. The writers can expand these duels into robust short stories or much longer works.

Challenges of the Scholarly Audience: The Scholarly Audience can be the most terrifying group ever. Hosts and writers often judge their own performances by the amount of laughter they hear, so a silent crowd often sounds like failure. There are a few ways to use this to your advantage, but you're going to need some talented writers to impress this type of audience.

How writers respond to the Scholarly Audience: Some writers clam up in front of these groups. Others thrive in the silence. If your writers have done some practice duels, they'll do much better in this type of environment. Practice gets writers comfortable with short time limits and gives them some resources for unguided work.

SWAGGER
BOOZE
DRAMA
GROW BRAIN STORM
DEME

fun
Crowd

Strategies for a Scholarly Audience show: Scholars like to laugh, but they'll be more impressed with well-crafted stories than with jokes. Your host should expect to start the event on time and to have a well-considered structure prior to the start of the show. Want to really blow them away? Run a rehearsal before showtime. Make sure the host knows exactly what to expect next.

While it's true that comedy pieces are the biggest audience pleasers at most shows, duelists don't need to be comedians to win this smart crowd. The Scholarly Audience revels in strong stories with fulfilling conclusions, multi-dimensional characters with full (albeit short) arcs, and well-considered metaphors.

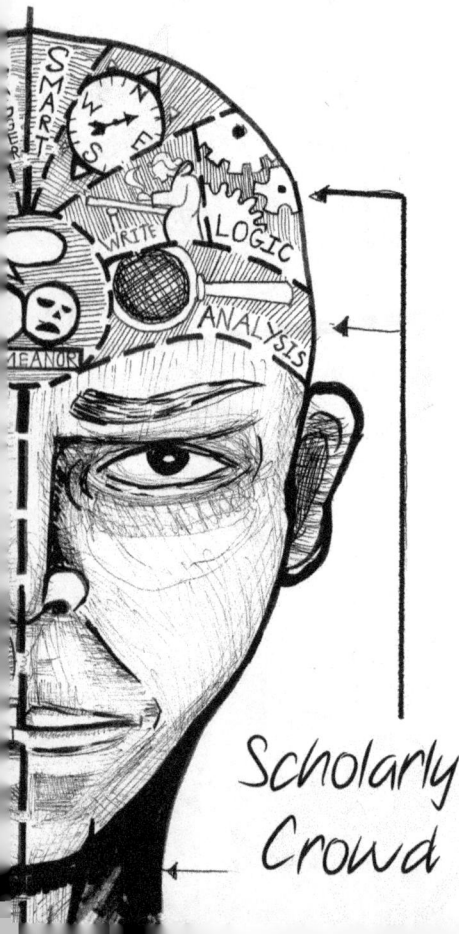

Scholarly Crowd

The Large Crowd

During the first three years, most of our shows welcomed audiences of 40 to 50 humans. We didn't welcome the three or four non-human guests who kept showing up, but try to stop them. Just try and see what happens, Sarah. It should be noted that shows of different sizes have totally different atmospheres. If your first writing duels have only five or six people in the audience, you've got to play to a very specific crowd. You're also much more likely to have a quiet crowd. The Large Crowd, which we could also describe as a "convention hall show," has more than 100 seats in the audience.

The Large Crowd will never have

the same feel as a small audience, so it makes sense to play bigger instead. I'm not saying we've ever hosted a show at a convention hall at a notable video gaming convention, but that's because we don't have a writing event. As the title says, The Ink & Blood Dueling Society doesn't exist.

All I'm saying is this. If you try to hold a regular writing duel event in front of an exceptionally large crowd, the screams of your audience will be drowned out in a sea of other voices. Your writers won't be able to hear everything, so you'll need to introduce a new element to the equation. Now, instead of a heckling audience, you introduce a host (or hosts) with a microphone for the crowd.

We've seen this work really well when we get the whole convention-hall audience up to the front of the room. We turn out the lights, make sure they're comfortable, and gently prod them into a story-hungry fervor. That last part usually happens with the help of a world-class hype man.

Benefits of the Large Crowd: Large crowds are fun because they bring a totally different type of energy than a smaller audience. There are more people, and it benefits our winning writer to have their recognition. It also helps us accommodate a growing audience.

Challenges of the Large Crowd: It's hard to find a middle ground of audience participation once you get to this quantity of people. We like when our audiences shout at the writers, but it loses its impact when the writers can't distinguish any particular message because of the noise. That's why we have an MC with a microphone walking around the audience. Everyone can shout, but our writers really focus on the people with the microphone.

How writers respond to a Large Crowd: Writing duels can be stressful, and they're even more so when you realize just how many people are reading your work. This isn't much different than any other show, but tell that to your stage fright. It doesn't care.

Strategies for a Large Crowd show: Set this up like a panel. Have your audience arrive first, then have the MC introduce the show. We keep a producer on stage, too. That's usually my job. I control who sees which story, and I scroll as the writers type. The writers, of course, are not introduced. They're kept hidden backstage, always within earshot of the audience and hosts. They should also be able to read the words that are being presented, so they can reference each other's work if they choose..

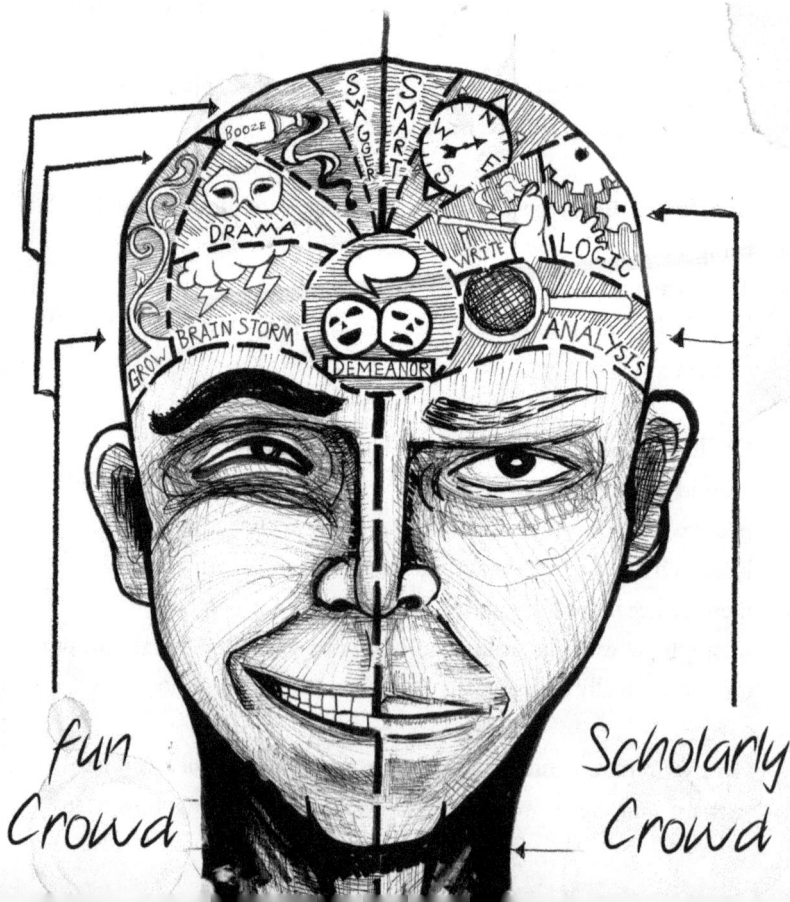

fun Crowd

Scholarly Crowd

Because Large Crowd shows draw so many people, only book the most talented duelists you can. These should be the winners of previous duels or professional writers who know how to quickly craft a story. Unlike with smaller crowds, Large Crowd shows pour all the audience's attention onto a single writer. If the writer bombs, the show will bomb. Don't tell your writers this, though. They already know.

Well, that's not entirely true about the quality of the writing. If you can get a witty enough MC and an energetic crowd, they should be able to handle less-compelling stories. Crappy stories demand ruthless attention. The people in the audience may end up mocking the characters or the choices made by the protagonist in the same way one might make fun of a B-List movie. Make sure your writers are aware of this possibility. Not everyone wants their first drafts to be publicly ridiculed for our entertainment.

So, how do you win at a Large Crowd event? First, listen and read. Then, be a masterful wordsmith. While you've got to be very talented to win at any of these events, the large-crowd event might be the toughest.

What happens if you lose a writing duel?

Oh, you don't want to lose a writing duel. There are stories about what happens to writers who have lost during these events. In some parts of the world, losing duelists are brought in front of the audience and quilled to death. Those practices are frowned upon by more progressive chapters, but they're not entirely gone. A quilling is a horrific thing to watch, but it's a celebrated part of the event's thousand-year history. At least that's what we tell the audience.

Another tradition we have is the slaps. In some chapters, writing duelists are slapped at the end of the event. Some chapters slap the losers, for they have brought shame upon themselves and upon their chosen profession. Others, strangely, unmask the winner and slap them instead. This perplexing tradition has deep roots, but their true origin is lost in time.

Most of the chapters of our clandestine writing society allow losing writers to slink away from their computers (or typewriters or quills) unscathed. We want our audience to celebrate the winners, but we don't want to disincentivize writers from competing in the first place. That's one of the major reason we insist on masks and costumes. Anonymous writers can do their best, and they're not penalized if they make a mistake.

Masked writers can also step away from their famed genres. If a well-known published author entered an event, he might be expected to stay within a specific style. His audience may feel dismayed if he strays into new areas or tests out new styles.

However, if we keep our writers hidden from the audience, if we don't advertise the competitors, anyone could be behind those words. Nobody needs to lose face because they tried one of our duels, and we like it that way.

Or more accurately, I like it that way.

Where do you host writing duels?

Don't over-think this at first. You just need a place to host a few writers. If you've never held a writing duel before, start small. You'll want to get comfortable with the actual feeling of what it means to complete a duel (ideally with a friend or two) and jump into larger events from there.

Don't worry about audiences when you start. Find a few writers first, then invite them to give it a shot with you. Everyone should have a laptop, if possible. Otherwise have at least one for every two people. Then, get comfy. You're going to do this yourself before you ask anyone else. Give your small group of writers some tea, then give them ten minutes and a one-word writing prompt. Maybe go for brunch after.

Or, once those ten minutes are up, give the writers a choice. Everyone is welcome to read their work, but nobody has to. If they hate what they've written, that's cool. That's your first duel. Get a few of these under your belt first. Then, talk to the writers about what they liked and what they didn't like. Remember, these

fig 27 a
Runes found off the
Coast of

practices are missing one key component of a traditional writing duel event. There's no audience, so nobody is shouting at them while they work and nobody's reading over their shoulder. These practices aren't competitions, either. Not really, anyway. You can all agree that one of you wrote the best story. That's not exactly the same as being unmasked in front of your adoring readers. Sometimes, it's even better.

Where to practice

When you're ready to hold some practice events, look for large, dry caves or writer-friendly coffee shops. These are the best places to blend in with the crowd, because there are always slews of incredibly-talented albeit undiscovered screenwriters using the spaces to work on their first great masterpiece. If you use one of these spaces, don't make a bunch of noise. You're there to write. Buy a drink, do your duels, and plot bigger and better things.

We've dueled in just about every coffee shop in Chicago, and there are definitely some things to consider when you choose where to go. First, know how many writers you have. If you're showing up somewhere with twenty-five people, you're going to need a hell of a lot more space than you'll find in most coffee shops. If you find a small doorway into a man's head, where you control his movements for a short time and get to live his life for him, maybe do that instead.

Next, find out where your writers usually like to get their stuff on paper. Some people use online platforms like Google Docs. That's where I'm writing these words right now. Others use non-internet based software like Scrivner. That's really helpful for formatting eBooks and print files. If everyone uses online platforms, you'll want a place with internet access. If nobody cares, you've got many more options. Hell, you could do this in the middle of the woods if your batteries can hold out for a few hours.

Remote practice: You don't have to be in the same room with someone to participate in a practice duel. If you have an internet connection, you can find your friends online to participate in remote challenges. We've done practice duels over Google Hangouts, and it works well. Online practice duels have the added benefit of shared documents. While you can choose to read your work aloud over your microphone, you could just as easily share your document with a friend so they can read it at their leisure.

Pen-pal practice: This is a form of remote practice reserved for the most patient of writers. Instead of using skype, you use the old-fashioned postal service. Don't forget to buy stamps. Or try homing pigeons. As long as you write small enough, this could be a very fulfilling way to interact with animals without having to see any other humans at all.

Where to host small events

You already know the answer to this. Start small, then expand. You could do this anywhere you want, and your choices depend on where you're located. If you want to host writing duels in a rural area, you'll have totally different options than we had in downtown Chicago. I'll share our story so you can see how we progressed, then I'll offer some ideas for those of you who don't have all the same resources available.

If the Ink & Blood Dueling Society existed

Even things that don't exist have to start somewhere. Let's pretend The Ink & Blood Dueling Society existed. If it started somewhere, it might have been a sports bar. That's where we didn't have our first practice.

We didn't call ahead. We didn't ask permission. We just showed up in masks. Two people brought computers and seven or eight people crowded around as the masked writers duked it out on screen. We didn't have a projector screen or connections for anyone else to watch. Sports played on the televisions in the background.

This wouldn't have worked for a large event, but it would have been exactly what we needed to get rolling. Our mismatched band of writers and audience members might have just showed up at the designated place at the designated time and rooted for a winner. People certainly would have bought drinks and tipped the wait staff. Then we would have left forever. We would never have held another duel there again.

Once we knew what it felt like to perform in public, our secret society might have wanted to secure a real space—one where our audience could be seated and watch without crowding the writers. We might have tried another sports bar next. We might have paid to use the back room of a bar in Logan Square. It might have drawn a similar crowd, and we might have treated it like a private event. You wouldn't have needed a ticket to get in. If you looked like you wanted to be there, you would have been welcome. At this new bar, we would have hidden two writers behind a curtain and hooked a third computer up to a big-screen television. The writers' work would have appeared on this big screen, high on the wall. That would have been the first time our whole audience could have seen everything that was being written.

That would have been a powerful moment. We would have booked our space and sent out invites to our friends. It would have been the first real writing duel event in Chicago. We also never would have held another duel there again.

After testing out two bars, we might have agreed to try something that better suited our audience. We might have considered ourselves a secret society, and we wouldn't have been too secretive if we used such a public venue. That would have been when we started looking at empty storefronts and theater spaces.

Eventually, we would have ended up at our favorite comic book store in the neighborhood. We liked the employees, and they were already familiar with neighborhood events. All three of our event's co-founders attended the store's game nights, where they set up tables and chairs for players every week. We might have asked to use their space, and they might have agreed to host us. They had internet, they had chairs, and their employees went out of their way to make us feel welcome.

If our secret society existed, that store would have been our first real home.

For this next bit, let's pretend it was.

Why use a comic book shop

We already loved this place. The comic shop drew a nerdy crowd, and their crew seemed to enjoy staying after regular business hours to play board games. They also seemed like the kind of readers that might enjoy a writing event. To top it all off, they were totally cool with costumes. We weren't the first group to enter the store in costumes, either. People dressed up to attend the store's Free Comic Book Day events.

The store also had all the chairs and tables we needed. They helped us set everything up for our first show, where we used two televisions to display the written words. I think one of the televisions was around 32 inches, the other was likely larger.

THE INK & BLOOD DUELING SOCIETY

PRESENTS A

WRITING DUEL EVENT

AUGUST 8, 1925 8:08 PM

EDGEWATER BEACH
HOTEL

We hid the writers directly behind the televisions, just behind a bookshelf, so they didn't have to appear directly in the audience's line of sight while they worked.

Then we set up twenty five or thirty chairs in front of the televisions. We also used a small table for beer in the back of the room. Guests could grab beer there, then watch the show from their seats. You'd have liked this setup. It was raw, unfinished, DIY. Totally your style.

Back then, we didn't really know how to organize a show. We started with six writers, and the first few events lasted at least four hours. Can you imagine anything lasting four hours? Not even Lawrence of Arabia is that long.

With six writers, we held seven rounds of duels. There were three preliminary rounds, each with two writers. Then we voted. The writers with the highest vote totals moved into the semi finals. The semi finals had two rounds as well, both with two writers. We voted again. This time, our two highest-voted writers moved onto the finals. I'm out of breath just describing it.

Don't get me wrong. We loved it, but it was tough to sustain a show that starts in the early evening and finishes thirteen years later. It's also worth noting that the writers varied in their abilities, and some rounds were much better than others. Audiences loved some events and fell asleep during others. It was an interesting time for our secret society. Some people stuck with us because of how clearly incredible our concept was while others, understandably moved on to other forms of entertainment that didn't require seven intermissions and a sleeping bag.

Note on comic book shops: Comic book stores have built in audiences, and that's super handy when you want to find people to come to a show. We were already part of this community. Because I was a game-night regular, it wasn't hard to make an announcement to people in the neighborhood.

For all you data science junkies, this is also a quick way to centralize a target demographic. The people who came to game night at the comic book store accidentally qualified for a few of our major demographics.

- They lived in the area or could easily get there.
- They enjoyed coming out to free events.
- They were nerdy enough to spend their free nights in a comic shop.
- Most of them could read.

Here's another fun fact. Retail locations tend to have nearby parking. Surprising, right? They also have lockable doors, regular business hours, and restrooms. These were all very helpful for a young secret society. We also benefited from the store's wireless internet. Because all of our writers crafted their stories in a cloud-based writing platform, we needed a reliable internet connection in order to make things work.

The other big part of working with a comic shop was the name recognition. When we advertised our event outside the shop, all we had to say was the name of a popular store in the city. Writers in other neighborhoods didn't have to memorize an address or write down any extra information. They could picture it as soon as we told them where to find us.

We eventually left that space, but it wasn't because we didn't like them anymore. After a year at the comic shop, we wanted to test out a setup that we devised much earlier. When we first came up with the concept of live writing duels, we figured out the most efficient way to show our work to an audience.

Unfortunately for us, there wasn't enough space for a projected show at the shop. Many of our events filled all the available seats, and we used televisions to show the writing. That meant an extra bulky setup and teardown process, even when we had a super thoughtful audience who helped with the process. We left that place and found an independent bookstore to sneak into at night.

Because we're not using a real theater, and because the shop donates their space for us, a community forms around each of these hubs. Attendees stay to help clean up. They purchase books from the host store. We don't have to ask them to do these things. It's just what happens when you work with your community. The event is better for everyone when everyone lends a hand. That's why we tend to produce our smaller shows in local businesses. That, and arenas haven't yet returned our emails.

Where we went next

We held our next writing events at an independent bookstore that also provided literacy services to people in our city. There were a few major differences between this bookstore and our friendly neighborhood comic shop. The first, and the most important reason for the shift, was our access to a projector.

When we first conceived of this idea, we planned to use three computers and a projector. Aside from chairs, that was all we really needed. Both writers could use their own computers, assuming everyone had internet, and we could connect the third computer to a projector to show their work to the crowd. The problem was, none of us could afford a projector.

That's why we set up televisions during our first year of writing duels. We had access to those things and we sure as hell weren't using them at home. They were heavy, sure. But they connected directly to our computers and we didn't need to bring a third computer. It wasn't a problem right away. Only when we started to draw larger crowds did people start to complain about visibility. From the back of the room, it became much harder to read any words at all.

Why use a bookstore

That independent bookstore became our home for the second and third years of our frequent meetings. They allowed us to use their projector. They also had a large projection screen and a fair number of seats. We eventually took over the children's section of the shop. We'd set up chairs before our events and tear them down again at the end. It felt secretive, though we maintained a robust online presence.

The bookstore offered more opportunities for expansion, and we made the most of them. I brought in a guitar player and, I'm not exactly sure how to describe this, a modern bard. With their combined efforts, we had a new intermission act to keep the audience entertained while we counted votes.

This was something we had talked about since founding the event, having entertainers. We just didn't know how to find them. When we finally did book acts for the intermission, it wasn't difficult at all. We were already a year into hosting one of Chicago's most intriguing literary events, and people were excited to attend. Curiosity turned out to be a major draw for our audiences.

Some of our guests, when asked how they learned of our secret society, told us they found the details online. When pressed to find out whether it was through a paid promotion on a large social network, these same guests demurred. Like sad vampires waiting outside after you have already closed the door, these guests hadn't been invited at all. Unlike vampires, they still came in to see us. Way to seize the day, random audience members.

Trying it outdoors

We've held writing duel events in many unlikely places. One of my favorites was a small art festival in a park on the northwest side of the city. Unlike the shows we held in bookstores, this one didn't allow alcohol. So, we left our beer sponsor behind. We had to figure out how to maintain the spirit of our event without computers, projectors, or electricity.

We didn't know who to expect. What are we, fortune tellers? It was entirely possible that nobody would show up to our little area, and we'd be left to entertain ourselves. We decided to bring our own notebooks, pens, and masks. We even made some crude signs to hang nearby, inviting others to come and duel with us. Then, we waited.

When the festival started, we quickly discovered that it was a family event. Most of our fellow duelists were children, and I don't mean grown ups who act like children. Many of our favorite audience members already fit that category, and we would have been excited to have them. Instead, a small horde of knee-nipping tikes strolled up to our notebooks and asked us to participate.

So, we welcomed it. We encouraged them to write with as much passion as they could muster. Some of them just wanted to play with our masks. Others seemed to like the sound of pens scratching on paper. It was a pretty strange experience, but it taught me how to organize our events without any technology at all.
The trick? Do the same thing that we did at the coffee shop.

Just have people write on whatever was handy. We gave them notebooks. Then, we gave them ten minutes. Everyone wrote independently. Nobody shouted. Nobody watched. Nobody even read over our shoulders. We just wrote for ten minutes as the festival happened around us. The wind blew our pages, and we got distracted by car horns, and once the timer went off, we shared our work. There wasn't any cheering, and we didn't have a loud audience.

It felt like writing in that coffee shop, way before we had ever come up with our first event, and that was just fine.

Where to host large events

We always planned to do this at conventions. That's why we set it up the way we did. One laptop for each writer. One laptop for the shared screen. One projector for the audience. That would allow us to host the event in a convention hall, in an auditorium, or in a movie theater.

I looked into movie theaters first. There are several small, independent movie theaters in Chicago. Those seemed like the places to go. So I stopped by and talked to one of the managers at the one in Logan Square. It didn't go well.

While most of the people I talk to about our event seemed excited to help, or at least excited to use us for publicity, the manager at the theater in Logan Square seemed completely ambivalent. She wasn't interested in working together, and I guess it's hard to blame her. We were a secret society, and I was just a lowly neighborhood writer.

It would have been really cool to work with the people at one of my favorite theaters to see our work appear on the big screen. I imagine lines to get in. Everyone would be waiting in masks and cloaks. People would chat about their expectations, about what surprises might be in store for them at such an unusual public event. We would have planned this show from the ground up. Four writers. Two sets of performers. Two hosts. A staged duel. A round of applause to determine the winner. Then once we had crowned a winner, a reception.

Instead, we brought it to conventions. That's what it was made for. While it would have been neat to partner with a local theater, we still brought it to huge audiences in Philadelphia and Boston. We wore masks. We performed rituals. And we got to see our writing on the big screen anyway.

My history with this event

I'm not the sole founder of The Ink & Blood Dueling Society. There were three of us. Our triumvirate, which I would have misspelled if not for the handy dictionary I carry with me at all times, all did an equal part in the creation of this group. We came up with the idea together. We held the first practices together. We organized the first real events together. I didn't take over as the main producer until 23 months later.

It's important to note that this didn't come from one person. It came from several people. Several writers. We shared it with our friends. A community formed around the events, and that's how this thing grew. It has never been one person's thing.

Your role in these events

If you're reading this book, you're either unusually interested in an eccentric writing event or you want to host one yourself. Scratch that. Those are usually the same thing. They should be. If you want to host writing events, you should be unusually interested in them.

Depending on where you live, most people won't know what the hell you're talking about when you mention writing duels. You'll find you quickly become accustomed to explaining the concept. You don't need to tell everyone about your group, especially if yours is a secret society like ours, but you will need to explain it to the writers you invite to participate.

Then, if you're anything like me, you'll find joy when other people start to explain it for you. When my friends or colleagues talk about writing duels, they usually turn to me for

Captain Jim Blood

an explanation. "You're the one who created these," they say, "Right?" In response, I turn toward any of the writers who have participated in the past.

Without exception, their explanations are always passionate and relatable. They've experienced the same joys in dueling that I've experienced, and I get to hear about it from a different perspective. It's also my way of nodding toward our secret society's roots. When someone mentions our supposedly secret event, my first response should always be to walk out of the room.

Wow, this chapter was supposed to be about your role in these events. Now, I'm spending the whole time talking about myself. Again. Rude.

Everything depends on you, but that will change if you do it right

Look, something will go wrong when you host your first event. That's alright. It happens to everyone. The key is your ability to adapt to the situation. We had seven-hundred-and-two things go wrong with our first event. Only fifty five went wrong the next time, and we called that a success. Since then, we've managed to minimize mistakes so only seven or eight things go wrong nowadays.

It's not so bad, messing up. When things go wrong now, we celebrate them. The first time we forgot a cord, we panicked. Oh no! We couldn't do the show if we didn't have this connection. The audience would get fed up with our lack of preparation, and they'd walk out the door on us. I was sure of it. The triumvirate didn't agree. One of our crew rushed to the store to find another cord before the show, and everything showed up on screen. Somehow, we managed to get out alive.

Another time, we forgot one of our computers. Can you imagine? We showed up to our own show, a show which requires only three computers for a group of 40 people, with a full 33% deficit in necessary technology. We were upset. We considered doing the show in a different format, having people crowd around our writers and shouting at them from behind. It worked when we tried it out at our first practice event, and it could have worked again. Instead, we decided to ask the crowd. Someone's hand shot up right away. They had a computer we could use. Of course they did. You can see what's happening here.

Everything centers on community. We're here to help each other out because we all want the same thing. The show must go on, but you don't have to go on alone. You just have to do all the work ahead of time.

Hey, that seems like a good time to talk about advertising.

THE INK AND BLOOD
Dueling Society
Presents a

Writing Duel Event
August 8, 1925 8:08 PM
Edgewater Beach Hotel

How do you advertise a writing duel?

Damn, that was a good transition.

Now you're wondering how a writing duel event, especially one that calls itself a secret society, gets people to come to their events. Here are a few strategies that worked for us. I'll start with the biggest ones, then work my way to the side strategies. Like many things in life, this seems to fall into the 80/20 rule. About 80 percent of our growth came from 20 percent of the things we tried.

Building a Network

Our biggest influx of audiences came when we introduced our event to people who had already organized themselves into groups. No, I don't mean gangs. That's absurd, and I'm a little upset you would assume that's what I meant. What I mean is hobby groups and live entertainment. People told us about other shows in the city and we went to see them. We made friends with the people putting on other shows, and we asked them to be in our show too.

Before long, we had joined other large groups of writers and performers. We found an existing community of people who spent their free time pursuing creative passions. We joined them, and they joined us. We advertised at the other major event that happened in the comic shop.

The store closed at 7pm every Thursday. Then, they brought out folding tables, chairs, and stacks of board games. These weekly events were exceptionally well attended, and I attended frequently. That was one of the first real community-oriented events I visited in the city. It's where we found the majority of our early audience.

When we started our secret society of writing duelists, I shared the invitation at game night. Some people weren't interested, but others jumped at the idea. We had a very strong showing at our first few shows. People didn't just come to the event, either. They shouted at our duelists, just like we asked them to. They participated as spectators and they participated as writers.

One of the people who worked at the comic shop even entered as a duelist. He rose through a challenging tournament during his first attempt, and he came out the winner. It was an unexpected delight to find so many talented writers in our community, and that was just the start.

It didn't take long before someone introduced a few theater producers to our show. I don't remember exactly how they heard about us, but they showed up in costume and cheered from the audience. This, I think, is what marketers call organic growth. Or maybe that's a botany term. Regardless, we weren't doing much to promote our events except holding them consistently and allowing the word to spread.

We did our best to maintain the secret aspects as well. Lord C. Byron Taylor printed business cards that contained nothing but our logo. It was a mysterious detail that accented the hidden nature of our events. I've used those cards to invite outsiders as soon as he gave me some of my own. The trick was to use the nearly-blank cards as little note pads. I gave the details of our events on the back of each card.

What a powerful moment, when you hand someone such a card. They're not likely to forget it, even if they don't make it to the show. It's the kind of thing that worked well for us, and I'd recommend it to anyone who wants to foster the same kind of exclusive feeling to their events.

The irony of these cards, of all of the marketing, is that we called ourselves a secret society. Our events are almost always open to the public. We never charge admission. One of the reasons we brought the duels to an art festival and several video game conventions was to increase access to communities that might not normally see this kind of show.

It still makes me smile when I think about it.

What do you need to produce a writing duel event?

There are only a few things you need to produce a writing duel event of your own. Here they are:

Three laptops.
Four writers.
A projector.
A screen.
A way to vote.

Well, that was a quick chapter.

Alright, you deserve more than that. This chapter might be the whole reason you bought this book, so we'll break down why we use each of these items and why you might not need to do the same. Let's start with the obvious.

What Do You Need to Produce a Writing Duel Event? (Part Two)

Laptops:

We have three laptops at each of our duels. Because only two writers compete at a time, we use two laptops for four or six writers. Then we have a third laptop connected to the projector at the front of the room.

These computers don't need to be very expensive. They don't have to be pretty or even very reliable. All they need are working keyboards and solid internet connections. If you have ethernet cords and a wall port, they don't even need wireless cards. Of course, it's harder to find a computer without Wi-Fi now, so don't get caught up in that. Just get three of the cheapest computers you can find and bring them to the event.

If your writers are the kind of people who already have their own laptops, you can even ask them to bring their own. We've done this in the past. It's a good habit just in case one of your computers breaks down, plus it gives writers a home-computer advantage. They'll already be familiar with the keyboards, and they won't be able to complain to you about having to learn to type on some new-fangled doohickey like a portable Bluetooth keyboard.

Some locations also have laptops available for borrowing or rent. Libraries especially may be able to work with you to provide the basic tools you need for a duel, just remember to work with your librarian to make sure you cause as little disruption as possible.

These events could thrive in a library setting, especially if you can pit one librarian against another. Have you seen librarians duel? They're ruthless.

A projector:

This is always the part that causes problems for first-time producers. Reliable projectors are expensive. So if the location doesn't already have one in place, this will be your biggest expense. We avoided the problem of projectors for as long as possible. We planned alternate strategies to show our work to audiences, and we asked our furthest audiences to stand if they couldn't see the screens.

Not all of you will have this problem. Some of you might literally be made of money. If you can pull a few hundred dollars off your sleeve, then you can exchange that currency for a good piece of technology. Problem solved. Maybe you peeled off a few dollars from your forearm to purchase this book. If so, thanks. That makes at least two of us who put ourselves into our work.

A screen:

You can project onto a wall, but if you're already going out of your way to get a projector you may as well take the last step. There are a few alternatives though. If you don't want to buy a screen, you could look for places with built-in projection surfaces. Offices often have white walls. Conference rooms have screens.

You can even make a screen of your own. Get a large roll of white paper and you can set this up just about anywhere. Imagine setting up your battery-powered projector in a subway station. Two of your friends unroll the white paper and plaster it over an advertisement on the wall. Someone sets up a wireless hotspot on their cell phone. Then, the laptops come out. You just created a guerilla writing duel—no screen needed.

A way to vote:

There are plenty of things you can use for voting tokens. This is the least important part of a writing duel event, because you can use audience applause to determine a winner. We used votes because the secret act of voting suited our theme and because one of the founders of our show had some nerdy voting tokens. If you want to use voting tokens, do so. Nowadays, we use a free online form to collect votes from our website. Did you notice how everybody has smartphones now? That makes this pretty easy.

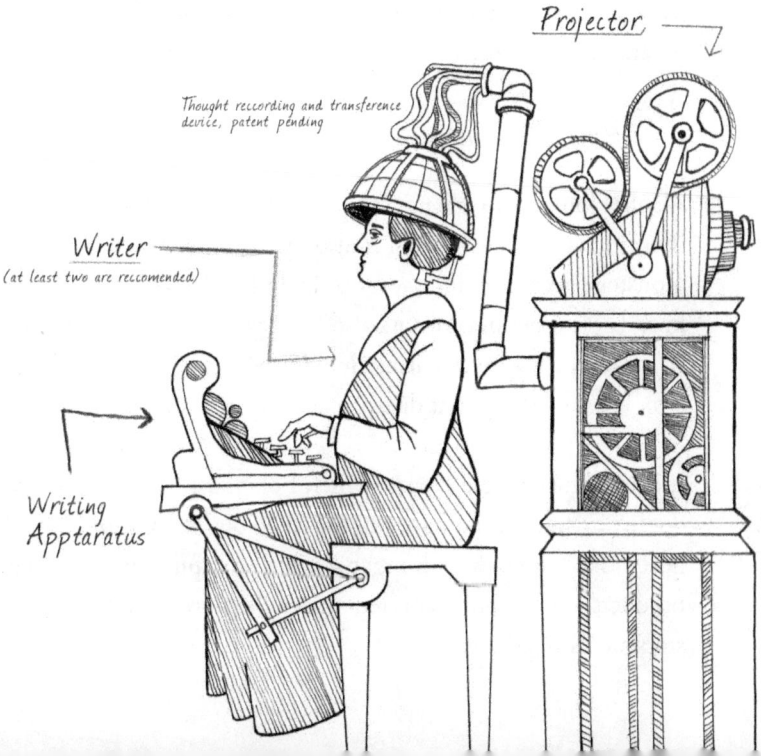

fig. 2
Material componets used in a traditional writers duel, circa 1887

Projector,

Thought reccording and transference device, patent pending

Writer
(at least two are reccomended)

Writing
Appataratus

Who sponsors a writing duel?

If you find yourself overwhelmed with the production duties that come along with putting on one of these literary shindigs, fear not. You don't have to do this alone. We've already talked about how community plays a major role for our group of writers. That's a symbiotic relationship. Here's where to look for sponsors, how to find the ones you want to work with, and how to win their affection.

Location:

Before you duel, you need a place to gather. You could use the alley behind your apartment building, but then you'd have to invite the 50,000 rats that normally dine there in the evenings. Instead, look for partners in your community. Find a spot that has some chairs, some walls, and fewer rats than writers. We've covered this in more detail elsewhere, so let's move on.

Libation:

Alcohol loosens people up, so they feel more comfortable shouting at helpless writers. It also makes some people into monsters. So if you don't want to include this part, that's totally fine. These types of sponsors also limit your audience to adults. If you're putting on a writing duel for wilderness scouts, maybe look for something that doesn't cause slurred speech.

If I held one of these events (which I obviously did not because it doesn't exist, etc.), I'd have only reached out to sponsors I liked. I never asked to work with organizations who put out poor-quality products, and I never expected any of them to help. That didn't stop me from asking.

I cold-called our first sponsor, then I set up an appointment to speak with their marketing person. I let them know what I wanted to talk about, and I was honest about my expectations. Candor keeps things simple. It saves you time. It saves your sponsors time.

Literature:

Your sponsors don't always have to provide something for your audience. They can help writers too. We found sponsors to donate their time and talents for every facet of our show. One of our sponsors runs a laser cutting service, and they've provided beautiful laser-cut awards for almost every one of our shows.

There's an interesting story there. Our friends with the laser cutter used my text (and some of my designs) to cut the awards. They took my work and laid it out. That's why, on the very first award we had cut, there was a typo. The winning writer noticed it right away, and everyone in the audience laughed. So we've included typos on many of our awards ever since.

The typos remind me of our roots, and they capture a moment in our duels that audiences often forget after the show. None of our writing duelists produce perfect results. There are typos on the screen. The readers sometimes read the typos aloud (though some readers kindly correct the words, if their intended meanings are clear).

How do you find sponsors for a writing duel?

You ask.

Why you need sponsors

If you're setting up writing duel events without any money, you may quickly realize how little you can provide for your audience. Unless you're very wealthy (and very generous), it makes sense to rely on the people who want to help.

Somewhere out there, a business wants to give you their stuff for your show. That feels nice. It's a validation of your work, and it's a benefit to your audience. It can be, anyway. We booked our first beer sponsor before we knew exactly what we were doing. The inclusion of craft beer at our events has since become a hallmark. I love the energy of a loose audience, and it makes me feel good to give them things for free.

Why you don't need sponsors

You don't need much to host a writing duel. If you have a couple writers, you should be all set. In fact, sponsors can complicate things. Sponsors need to be advertised and, while they often

Fig. 287
Shield Crest

provide their own marketing materials, that's one more thing to set up before your show. If you don't have a sponsor, don't let that slow you down. Get started without them.

This is your show. Don't wait for someone to give you permission to start writing.

The economics of theater

Someone is more qualified to address this than I am. I can only tell you how we organized our events and why we chose to do what we did. We wanted to create an inclusive community, one that didn't cost anything to attend. As such, we didn't pay anyone for anything. We booked our spaces, mainly, for free.

We worked with businesses to find locations that could be mutually beneficial, but really, everyone who helped with this event did so for the good of the event. Our business partners and sponsors have not recouped their costs. Our writers, hosts, and producers didn't make enough from donations to even go out for dinner.

It wasn't created to be a business. Our society of writing duelists was made to be a participatory and inclusive event. Anyway, here's why you might want to charge for tickets and why you might not.

The case for ticket sales

Writers deserve to be paid. So do hosts, producers, and the people who work at the venue you use. If you choose to charge audiences for tickets, you'll have a budget to work with. You can pay your writers for their time and develop a cadre of talent that will stick around from one event to the next.

You might even be able to hire a full-time ringer. If you find a writer who always does impressive work, you could secure their time and make it worth their while. This business could grow and you could create a valuable job in the entertainment industry, something that would be more than just an honor.

While that's an enticing idea, we decided against it. Here's why.

The case against ticket sales

Theater doesn't need more ways to limit audiences. When's the last time you stepped into a theater? Audiences are old and wealthy. They have venues. They have shows. They have whole theater companies that cater directly to their needs. If you want to start a theater company, do so. If you want to host writing duels, consider opening up your events to everyone.

Our events are always more fun when there are new and unique voices in the crowd. We don't want everyone to look or sound like me. Nobody wants that. Our writers, our producers, and our hosts should come from everywhere. Taking money out of the equation allows us to welcome a much grander audience.

Because we were working for free, it didn't feel weird to ask other people to do the same. We weren't telling writers that they should write for exposure, or that they would have something to put on their resumes. That's what horrible businesses do when they want something for free. Our group wasn't a profit machine. It was a live, theatrical, literary event. And we had people lining up to help.

You'll have to weigh these concepts for your own event.

Formatting a show for writing duels

Anyone can host a writing duel. In this section, we'll talk about a few of the most important lessons that came from our first few years of production. In case you're skipping around this book (because you're in a hurry or because you don't understand how to read a book), I'll give you a short explanation about to expect in the next few pages. This segment includes tips and tricks. For a foundational guide, check out the earlier chapters.

Timing is everything

Our first events lasted four hours. Think about that. Some incredibly kind comic store employees agreed to stay late to watch the shop as our ragtag group of writers took over. They gave us free reign to set up chairs, to move televisions, and to hand out free beer to dozens of guests. How did we repay them? We invited six writers to compete in a needlessly complex tournament of duels.

Now, we take our time instead of rushing and the whole event takes less than two hours. We even brought in musical acts and comedians. Those extra talents spiced up the show when we counted votes and re-engaged the audience.

Finding entertainers to fill the gaps

Our dueling events have a few specific moments of downtime. Specifically, we need to keep the crowd entertained while we count votes. When we first started, we just told everyone to take a break. "Grab a beer and hang out," we said. So that's what they did.

THE
PERFORMERS

Audiences don't have trouble milling around, but it can be tough to bring everyone back. That's why we started bringing in outside entertainers. We've tried all sorts of acts, and all of them can work. We're lucky to have many talented people in the city, and there are tons of different styles to choose from.

We brought in a comedian, and he entertained us by commenting on our event as an outsider. "It's like I walked into the nerdy version of Eyes Wide Shut," he said. He pointed out how weird it was to see so many people in masks hanging out at a bookstore, and then he did some of his regular bits. It went over well.

We also brought in a juggler. The juggler wasn't quite up to snuff, and it the audience politely clapped at the end of the performance. Even with an amateur act, we accomplished our goal. The audience stayed engaged with the show, and our host was able to maintain the energy of the show without a fifteen minute break between each round of duels.

My Favorite Entertainers

After spending the day catching up with a friend, I was waiting at the Brown Line when I spotted Vinny. We knew each other because of a shared experience at a theater company in the city. He's a local celebrity in that community, and I'm always happy to see him. That day was no exception.

We rode the train together and went to a friend's housewarming party. There, we drank with friends. We met Ross too, another member of the theater company. Ross and Vinny aren't brothers, but they act like they are. They both have larger-than-life personalities. When I picture Vinny, I always imagine him with a handle of whiskey at his side. He shares this bottle with all of his friends, and he entertains them with stories. Vinny is good with people.

If Vinny always has a bottle of whiskey, Ross always has a guitar. Like Vinny, he shares with everyone around him. He plays for his friends, and we're lucky to have him around.

On the night of the housewarming, I found myself a unique situation. Instead of being surrounded by people, as both of these talented entertainers often were, they just had me. Ross played his guitar. Vinny used the music as a backing to tell a story. He spoke with a rehearsed pace, and I hung on every word.

The enormity of these talents astounded me I felt like the luckiest person in the city to be the sole audience member at a private event with my two favorite entertainers. That's why I invited them to perform at the next of our writing events.

They've been performing with us ever since.

In conclusion

You already have everything you need to participate in a writing duel. You have the know how and, with a little luck, you'll have some good people to help you along the way. If this guide has a theme, it's this: When you encounter a challenge during the process, the answer almost always lies in your community.

We couldn't have created our event without support. Our friends built this. They're the reason we keep it going, and we encourage you to give it a try. After all, you can't be a part of our event. Our clandestine cadre of writing duelists doesn't exist, so nobody can be a part of it. Get it?

CharlesHuthDesigns.com